CHANGE
YOUR
BRAIN
CHANGE YOUR
LIFE

-The Great Ideas Generator-

Change Your Mindset –Think Differently

Unleash Your Inner Potential, Learn How To Use Your Brain More Effectively

---

TABLE OF CONTENTS

INTRODUCTION

Congratulations on purchasing The Great Ideas Generator: Unleash Your Inner Potential, Learn How To Use Your Brain More Effectively, and thank you for doing so.

The chapters in this book will be discussing the importance of creativity and new ideas in life. We all are creative in our own way, but only a few of us know about the importance of creativity. It is beneficial in life if you want to generate brand new ideas. It also happens at times that your creative mind goes in the hibernation period, and that, in turn, results in various unsuccessful ventures of life. All that you need is to learn some basic strategies for keeping your creative mind alive. So, I have tried to provide you with a comprehensive guide for dealing with the various barriers in your mind that come between your creative aspect and reality of life. Also, as you unleash your creative mind for new ideas, it can bring in new lights of happiness and satisfaction in your life.

You will also find out certain practices for your daily life that can help in generating ideas much easier. Well, when I talk about practices, they are nothing fancy and are very casual and general in structure. You will also need to alter your view of creativity and mindset. So, keep on reading this book and you will soon be able to be a great generator of new ideas.

There are plenty of books on this subject on the market, thanks again for choosing this one! Every effort was made to ensure it is full of as much useful information as possible. Enjoy!

CHAPTER 1
UNDERSTAND THE IMPORTANCE OF ACTIVELY PROMOTING CREATIVITY AND INNOVATION

No matter what aspect of life we talk about, there are two things that can do wonders and are also considered to be very important. Yes, we are talking about creativity and innovation. These two can be regarded as the key to new ideas, new life, new achievements, new goals, and many others. In short, innovation and creativity, when combined together, can act as the magic spell for success in life. What is innovation? It is the overall process of giving birth to and implementation of a new idea. Innovation is the process of collecting all the useful forms of ideas in one place and then converting all of them into new useful products, processes, methods, or services.

All of these ideas are the overall result of creativity, which is often regarded as a prerequisite for the process of innovation. It is the capability of combining various in a completely unique way or making useful associations among the ideas. Creativity can easily provide new nature of ideas for improving quality in the organizations and finally, innovation successfully puts all of these ideas into action. Innovation and change can be related closely, although both are different from each other. Change involves a better and new form of ideas. The new idea might be the building up of a new process or product or it might also be the idea of changing the very way in which something is being carried out. In large-sized businesses, change and innovation are both necessary for satisfying the beneficial stakeholders.

Innovation and Its Strategic Importance

For both the new organizations as well as established organizations, change and innovation tend to be beneficial in a changing and dynamic environment. Whenever any organization fails in properly carrying out the change and innovation as required, its employees, customers, and also the community can suffer a lot. One needs to learn to properly manage change and innovation.

Innovation and Its Types

There are three types of innovation:

- **Technical:** It involves the creation of new services and goods. Most of the technical form of innovations take place through proper research and also development efforts, which are intended for satisfying the demands of the outer world where everyone is always looking out for something new, faster, better, or innovative.

- **Process:** It involves the creation of new methods for distributing the already existing ideas or services.

- **Administrative:** It takes place for better supporting the production, creation, and delivery of the services.

All types of innovation work together. For instance, the fast development of the normal form of business to e-commerce shows process innovation. But, this very new process needs various technical innovations in the sector of technology. Also, as a business shift to e-commerce, innovation in the administrative sector is also required. It is often said that 'Doing anything new indicates doing something in a different way.' So, it can be said that change and innovation actually work hand in hand.

Innovation and Technology

Technology is often described as the application of knowledge related to science for a new service, process, or product. It is also referred to as the systems, processes, methods, and skills for transforming all the resources into useful services. It is actually embedded in each and every service, product, procedure, and process. Whenever you find a better form of process, product, or procedure for doing any kind of task, you have innovation. Process innovation is the change that can affect the methods of output production. Technological form of innovations is daunting in structure because of its complexity and also the pace of change. It is often considered as beneficial for adding an advantage to the competitive aspect. As there is development in technology, the obsolescence of products is most likely to increase, and thus, products with innovation need to be introduced to the markets.

Benefits Related to Innovation

Innovation does come with a series of benefits along with it. Let's have a look at them.

Reduced Costs and Improved Productivity

There is a majority of process innovation, which is all about reducing costs. This is generally achieved by bringing some improvement in the flexibility or capacity of the business for allowing exploitation of the scale economies. As you reduce the costs, you can easily focus on the long-term goals of your business. The primary goal should be to look around for various ways in which the waste can be eliminated. This could provide you with an increased level of competitiveness.

Better Quality

Better quality of services and products will help in meeting the needs or requirements of the customers. When innovations are marketed effectively, it can result in improving the level of profits and sales. When you invest some of your time, along with money for innovation, customers will learn to value them.

Boosting the Position

Innovation can help in anticipating the changes in the market easily and thus can get you much ahead of the opportunities. So, it can help you in properly reacting to the shifts instead of forced shifts. You will also able to differentiate yourself from the competition. This form of innovation can be brought about by analyzing the trends in the market, by listening properly to the suppliers and customers and by studying the moves of the competitors.

Improve Relations

When you have an innovative form of workplace, it turns out to be really stimulating for all the employees. When you cultivate pride in all your services and also have an ardent desire for making the company the leader in the industry, can help in boosting productivity and also reduce turnover in the workplace. This can result in more success for the business as employees are often regarded as the primary source of innovative ideas. Always try to listen to them for bringing about a change, and it can also help in improving the relationships with them. You can also ask them for their feedback in various areas such as marketing, efficiency, and also services. They are the ones who can provide you with honest reviews.

Creativity and Its Importance

Creativity can do wonders. It is very essential for any type of organization when you really want to improve the growth of your business. Many organizations today have opted for cool and creative surroundings for the employees in the workplace, which can help them in relaxing and sparking the creative nature of thinking for getting done with new ideas. One of the best ways of getting 100% of the employees is by supporting open-mindedness and also by setting up an inspirational environment.

Thinking Right Outside the Box Can Provide Wonderful Results

Why is it essential to broaden our mental horizons? When you think outside the box, you can generate passion, excitement, and also creativity. There are times when teamwork turns out to be very important for giving birth to new ideas along with solutions, as two or three heads are always profiting than one. We tend to perform much better as we collaborate. We look out for the primary need of humans, and that is a connection that can effectively activate our hearts. As you look at it from the perspective of decision making, just imagine the number of decisions and ideas that you will be able to collect by setting up a creative environment where human minds are actually encouraged for thinking with their own capability.

Treat all your team members like creative beings and listen to what they say. You also need to support them properly for developing their very own imaginations. You can feed in creativity simply by questioning. In order to give birth to new ideas, you are required to develop the required space and also support that kind of culture and behavior.

Dopamine, Creativity, and Curiosity

When your brain is exposed to the stimulus of reward, the brain responds by effectively increasing the release of dopamine which is a neurotransmitter and is often connected with motivation, pleasure, and movement. With proper rewards, your team members can easily come up with several creative ways of bringing about an improvement in the workplace, solve the problems easily, and foster their own imagination. As you increase the imagination, it can result in the creation of more possibilities and also can also allow you to reach for and accomplish brand new goals. Creativity can also give rise to curiosity that can easily drive the very desire to learn new things. It can open up your mind to all those paths which are not explored yet.

Solving the Problems with Creativity

When creativity is being fueled up by passion, you are required to focus on the development of individual talents for expressing creativity and also for having all your team members reach their best potential. When there is a lack of this form of action, the team members are most likely to get disengaged from your organization. They will soon start to feel undervalued as you are not using their strengths and talents. They might also feel tired and bored. But, how to get started with this?

- **Creative environment:** You need to create a workplace environment that can easily encourage creativity. For this, you can start decorating the workplace with fresh, bright colors. The main motive is to provide the members with a sense of ownership.

- **Work hard and play even harder:** You need to start allowing your team members to play. You can opt for flip charts, colored markers, paint, music, Lego, or anything that can help in sparking the process of creativity at the time of brainstorming sessions.

- **Brainstorming:** You can set a meeting for brainstorming and working on a project or solution. This will provide your team with the right form of intention right before entering a meeting.

- **Setting up goal board:** You need to set up a board where you can place all the strategies and goals that your organization is actually striving for. Try focusing on one single goal every week or solution for working on.

- **Teamwork and homework:** You can start giving your team some kind of pre-work where you have a goal for the specific meeting. Ask your team members to come up with one solution or suggestion for your problem or goal.

- **Rewarding creativity:** Follow with a great reward for the best form of solution or suggestion that all the members of your team have agreed upon. This is equally important as any form of implementation of an idea or suggestion.

- **Establishing an engaging form of rewards:** You can opt for incentives such as wine bottles, movie tickets, money, voucher, or anything else. You need to establish engaging rewards so that the members get encouraged to work more with their creative minds.

What Can You Actually Gain By Promoting Creativity in Your Workplace?

Development of creative culture actually takes a lot of time, and it starts with the management, being less judgmental to all the suggestions that you receive from the team, and having an open mind. It is often said, 'Patience is a virtue'; you are required to provide some time to all the members of your team for developing creativity within the organization and also for putting together all their ideas in order to look out for the optimum solutions. Most of the team leaders are always expected to think in a creative way and also come up with some sort of innovative solutions for the problems of the organization. However, by properly cultivating and then using up the creative abilities of the members of your team, you will be able to give birth to even more useful forms of creative solutions and ideas for the problems of the organization.

But do you know exactly why? It is because every one of us tends to think in a different way. A diverse nature of the group possesses a wide range of perspectives along with the knowledge and this again goes back to why more heads are always better than one. The benefits that you can get from creativity in your workplace are actually countless. Let's have a look at some of them.

- Increased nature of the interaction

- Increase in engagement

- Increase in passion

- Increase in motivation

- Increase in productivity

- Improvement in problem-solving abilities

- Improvement of self morale

Drawbacks of Putting Aside the Creative Side

There are many people who are still in proper touch with their creative side. As we start growing older, many of us decide on going in for a creative career choice. But, for those who do not take up that path, their level of creativity can decline significantly as adulting takes over. This, in actual, is not at all a good thing. Creativity that is not being used is not benign in nature. It eventually transforms into rage, grief, judgment, shame, and sorrow. Humans are creative beings. We all are creative by nature. It is to be noted that the creative aspect won't disappear permanently. You are only required to keep on exercising all those muscles of creativity for getting them back to action.

Also, not being able to nurture the creative side can also result in added stress in life, problem in feeling mindful, loss of concentration, and others.

Creativity and Its Benefits

Creativity does come along with a long list of benefits. Let's have a look at them.

- **The feeling of pride:** 'Yes, I did that.' This is the best thing about being creative. It is actually nice to spend some hours of your day creating something and as it is done, it can easily reflect your inner personality and creativity. It is actually a great expression of yourself. Also, there is also a great sense of joy that comes along with pride.

- **Reduced anxiety, stress, and mood swings:** It has been found from various studies that a creative form of engagement can effectively reduce stress, mood swings, and depression. Also, as you engage in any form of creative activity for once in a day, it can nurture your positive state of mind as well. Opting for creative activity is actually very easy, so there is nothing to worry about. You can start with doodling, playing guitar, crafting, redecorating the kitchen, etc. you are most likely to reduce your daily stress that arises from work pressure.

- **Ability to solve problems faster:** As you turn out to be creative, you can become a bit more creative and resourceful for finding the things out just like you need while creating something. You can open up your mind and concentrate only on the solutions.

- **Stress relief:** We all feel anxious or stressed at some point in our life because of work, family, or something else. As you absorb your soul in any kind of creative activity, you can easily wash off the dust of daily life from your soul. It might only last for a short while, but it can provide you with an amazing feeling.

CHAPTER 2

DISCOVER WHY CREATIVITY STAGNATES SOMEWHERE BETWEEN CHILDHOOD AND ADULTHOOD

Are creativity and age connected to each other? Yes, they are. Creativity is, most of the time the only domain of the young and it is also true only to a certain extent. The decline in creativity does not actually start as human beings reach the age mark of 45 or 50. It actually starts at the age when we start going to school. At the age of 5 or 6, human beings use about almost 80% of the creative potential that they possess. Human beings at that age tend to invent something daily, no matter whether that very invention has been made before or not. The fact that works here is that we start innovating at a very remarkable rate. The scary part now comes in; by the age of 12, we have already lost about 2% of our creative potential and it is also going to stay for the remaining part of our lives.

Why Are Younger People Much More Creative Than the Adults?

Children and younger individuals tend to have a more powerful imagination when compared to adults. This is mainly because the younger people are much less constrained by their very own thought patterns. As people start being good at their life, they have the tendency to develop all those habits that can actually serve their purpose and them very well. All of these habits are the styles of thoughts that actually work. As we keep on accumulating the techniques of our thoughts, there are three things that happen.

First, we turn out to be more effective in nature and are also capable of mindlessly navigating the tricky waters.

Second, we start adapting to all the norms of the society along with the accepted paths of thinking. Thus, making us much more effective with the society in which we live along with the people.

Third, we tend to be the only prisoner of our very own success. Only sticking to what actually works out makes us less creative and also more successful. What is the need of being random while you can actually be right? But, unfortunately, what actually works is only those things that worked in the past, missing all those enigmatic nature of paths that can lead to surprises that are not expected at all.

The Actual Price of Acceptance

We soon start to learn the required price of staying alive in this modern world, and that is conformity. For living with several other people, we are required to follow all the values and rules, which most of the time seems to be much more about what we cannot do rather than what can be done by us. We tend to be straight-jacketed right into doing what is done by others instead of reinventing the world in which we live daily. As someone tries to be creative, they might also turn out to be very unpredictable; this can make the whole act of living with such people a threatening and uncertain kind of experience. So, what we are always taught is to be nice to people along with being polite instead of not scaring others with our creative aspect of mind.

The schools play a deep part in drilling in conformity inside us. We come to learn that there is only one way of true thinking. We also come to learn that every question comes with only one correct answer, and this thing is also instilled in the minds of the teachers. Success in life is based on finding out what is actually wanted rather than what is actually interesting. In examinations, we are asked to read all the questions. The marks are awarded for that one single correct answer and regurgitation and nothing for the lateral way of thinking and creative mind.

The universities are actually worse than our high schools which tend to be worse than the junior schools. At the level of the university, we only learn to provide a reference to all the assertions. We never or rather we cannot question the top-notch knowledge and wisdom of the professors. As we leave the path of education, we have already been converted into the functional beings of society, suffocating or rather killing our creative potential. You might start thinking that academic knowledge is actually bad in nature which is not the case at all. The majority of it is actually interesting in nature and we can also use them in various ways. The only thing is that as we learn to repeat the same knowledge that we have acquired, there is very little or almost no form of creativity in it.

Adulthood and the Traps

As we grow into adults, we tend to be less creative by nature but not at all in a traditional way. Our continuous decline in creativity is much more because of getting trapped in the cognitive holes than fading away of old age. Creativity tends to fade away as we start not using it or not paying much attention to it. It is often said, 'Use it or be ready to lose it.' The primary culprit for this is the natural pattern of human habit.

As we start doing something in a way, we tend to get comfortable with it and thus show up zero efforts in varying it or changing the path. For example, we try to find the best road for reaching our home and we make it a habit to drive only in that way, no matter if it is clear of even completely blocked with traffic. We also slowly grow the habit of getting stuck in familiar nature and cliché conversations. The majority of us are too busy to read; only a few of us still carry on with our study and only a few of us innovate still just for taking the fun of it.

The Trap of Experts

Many of us opt for studying to become experts. But, we can still fall in the trap of experts where we might have the tendency of only protecting and defending our hill in place of building it taller. We tend to repeat the same thing in the organizations as well. Suppose, when you are the manager of an organization, you will be having the attention of all those who are below you. It is actually a lot easy to start thinking that all those who are below you are trying to take over your wisdom and intelligence.

It is actually a huge trap for feeling obliged to all the knowledge expectations that are put upon you by others. This very cycle keeps on going, even at home, where our parents tend to take up the same kind of role, only being the great source of knowledge for the children, who only know that as they are adults, they are not at all meant to be creative and certain with things.

Unintelligent Closure

Intelligence is often related to creativity, to some extent. It is thought that people who are bright have the ability to be more creative by nature. But, bright people also have the tendency to fall into the expert trap. Another great reason behind this is that the bright people tend to close their gateway of thinking very quickly which is mainly because of their capability of getting things right within seconds. So, they just stop thinking and thus drawing in a barrier for their creative mind.

Keeping Alive Your Creativity

The primary secret of life is being able to keep up with the creative aspect of your mind. As long as you can allow your juices of creativity to flow freely, you will be able to always stay much ahead of the lot. One of the best ways of removing any kind of barrier in your way of creativity is by doing different types of things in life. Start by reading various newspapers and books. You can opt for traveling places for your holiday. Keep on talking with different people, listen to what they say, and just opt for synthesizing and synergizing.

Just don't lose any of the opportunities of regenerating your powers of generation. But, what can you do for the aging effects on your life? Human beings are born with a settled number of brain cells.

The brain cells tend to die right after the age of 50 and the speed increases by the age of 70. This might be true but keeping aside any form of mental illness, this is much smaller when compared with the effect of habitual ossification. All those who have been creative all throughout their lives are much ahead of others, not only those individuals who are older than them but also the ones who are younger when compared to them. With continued practice, you can learn to be better at your own creativity. It has also been found that creativity can directly affect longevity. All those who live active mentally rather than just being active physically live longer than others. If you decide to go to the gym of your mental creativity every day, the alertness that you are going to develop can help you in living longer.

CHAPTER 3

LEARN HOW TO RE-AWAKEN DORMANT CREATIVITY TO HELP YOUR BUSINESS ACHIEVE MORE

Creativity is that aspect of life that most people think other people possess in them. The entrepreneurs and business owners might also think that being creative is an act that can be applied only by all those people who are associated with arts such as writers, painters, and musicians. But in actual, all those businesses that are successful today or are able to grow in the way they wanted and also evolve with time, it is only because of the creative side of the employees along with the owners. When you try to be creative, it is not only about the artistic pursuit. It is actually a must as you try to make your business thrive and grow in this world of today. So, I have compiled some of the ways in which being creative can help you in making your businesses grow along with certain tips for sparking the creative side of yourself.

Why Is Creativity so Important for the Growth of a Business?

Creativity is most of the time attached to the growth of a business. But, the majority of organizations have the notion that they are not creative enough. A study was conducted with all the winners of the Cannes Lion award for growth in advertising and marketing. In the study, the winners were evaluated by using three factors: The number of awards won by them, the categories in which they won, and also consistency, which was based on the total number of years for which the organization has been winning awards.

Those companies which scored the most in the aspect of creativity in accordance with the study were also found out to possess the highest net value, the highest percentage of revenue growth of organic nature, and the highest return for the shareholders. Another survey was also conducted for gauging the assessment of people's creativity along with growth in business. That survey also produced the same results. More than 80% of the leaders of business along with the decision-makers, agreed that what allowed them to grow in business was creativity that made their business gain so much profit such as in revenue growth and improved share in the market.

One of the primary reasons why being creative is actually so beneficial for business growth is that it can effectively provide the businesses with a definite way with which they can easily set themselves much apart from others. Once you have acquired for your organization all those things that make it new and also different when compared to others, it can successfully stand out in the crowd of competition, build up a loyal base, attract the attention of brand new customers, and also develop returning customers.

How to Re-Kindle Your Creativity?

One of the common mistakes that people tend to make is to think of creativity as innate and not like a skill that can actually be developed with time. People have the habit of frequently saying things in addition to this line, 'I am not creative.' When you say that you are not at all creative is more or less like as you do not know Spanish or you haven't yet read the new novel yet. It is actually a temporary state of human beings. Being creative can be learned. The primary step that you are required to take is to ask some questions to yourself that are related to all the problems and difficulties that your business is facing right now.

For starting, you can ask, 'How can someone differentiate my organization from the competitors?' All that you need to do now is to rephrase it or rework it. As you do so, you will be able to reach out to the problem from a completely different perspective and also come up with a new solution for the very problem.

Creativity often needs connecting all the dots between various things that do not actually seem to together in any aspect. One of the ways of starting to see all the connections between your ideas and things is by letting yourself to explore all the activities and interests that actually interest you. But, all such things might not even have anything to do with the aspect of your business. All the people that you meet, experiences, books, and articles that you read might not have any form of a direct link to your business now. But, sometime in the coming future, you might need to just have a look at your past experiences and get some idea for taking your business to the upcoming level.

Accepting Your Creative Side

You will come across some people in your life who will be informing you willingly that they are creative by nature, while there are others who think that they have it by birth, or they think that they are not creative at all, and you are not as well. The actual truth is that everyone in this world is creative in their own way. It is possible to improve one's creativity in several ways such as exercise, diet, and also practice. Creativity is like a pathway that can help you in knowing about yourself better and for creating a proper balance in your present life.

If you start thinking of creativity in a way that is not something that people are gifted with, you will be able to place yourself better for finding the creativity inside yourself. When you do not permit yourself to explore the creative side, it is more or less like freezing a part of your own self and also not agreeing to the tranquil and therapeutic focus that comes along with creativity.

Staying Inquisitive

If you really want your mind to start thinking in a creative way, you are required to start paying attention to all those things that you generally overlook or do not pay enough attention to. If you only notice the forest with no attention to the twigs and leaves, you are actually losing out a great amount of learning and beauty. Start learning one new thing per day by asking yourself a brand new question. All that you need to do is to stay inquisitive.

Staying Imaginative

Imagination can do wonders. It is like a pair of invisible wings that can allow you to fly. You will be able to fly in your universe of infinity. If you tend to have the power of imagination, you are capable of going for a world trip while having your lunch. Wouldn't it be possible to give birth to a great story- Around the world in 15 minutes? You just need to find various ways in which you can easily express your imagination. You can start by writing journals and let the pen be the wings that will allow you to fly in your world of imagination. You can also opt for writing stories or doodling. Try to make imagining a daily habit.

Staying Inspired

Try to identify your very source of inspiration and make sure that you visit it every day. When you think of inspiration, it could possibly be anything, a person, a tree, or even a dog. Just ensure that you are having the required amount of inspiration fuel for letting your creative juices flow freely.

Changing Perspective

You must have heard about this common phrase, 'Think outside the box.' Well, doing this thing is actually very important for sparking up the creativity in your mind as it will allow you to see every situation from a completely different angle. As you try to change your perspective, you need to approach all the problems by simply breaking them into several small elements. After that, shuffle all the elements and try to look for some new ways of looking out for solutions. This method can help in enhancing your creativity as it helps in removing any nature of fixations that might be hindering your creativity.

Being Inventive

Try giving small tasks to yourself, such as small fun projects that can help in stimulating the brain and thus present it with brand new challenges. A creative mind is somewhat like a huge bag of small-sized random information. The quality of all those things that you will be able to take out of the bag depends completely on the quality of things that you will be putting inside. The main job of creativity is to set up a better future. So, try to keep all your interests numerous. Try to invent something new, even though it has already been invented.

No individual in this world knows everything. So, you can come across new things every day and invent something new. Keeping your mind open to all forms of possibilities can do wonders. Explore. Paint. Read. Ponder. As you keep on putting various types of things in your mind, you will be able to enhance the power of your creativity. When you come along with an inventive mindset, you will also be able to invent some new ways of solving the problems that your business is going through. So, what are you waiting for? Open up your mind and be creative.

CHAPTER 4
EXPLORE WAYS IN WHICH WE CAN WORK TOGETHER TO KEEP CREATIVITY ALIVE FOR EVERYONE

Most of us face a very common problem today: we tend to get weighed down by all our mundane tasks along with urgent projects including the tricky spreadsheets. The end result? We tend to feel less inspired and thus less creative. It is actually a very sad nature of the cycle that most of us encounter in our daily lives. But when can we break the cycle? Well, the right time for breaking it right now. We need to keep on working together on our creative aspects for not permitting our lives to turn into a fixed form of routine. Let's have a look at some of the ways of dealing with this.

Offering Space for Sharing Knowledge

We need to utilize all the skills along with the expertise of our team members for keeping alive creativity in all. There is actually no form of shortage of intelligence or talent within the team; it is just waiting for being passed on. Try encouraging all your people to share all that they know and what they are able to do along with their fellow teammates. This will help all the members of your team to invent a brand new interest or rather a passion that they will be able to learn more or develop the skills for it. They will also be able to use the same for their very own roles. You can ask your team members to share their skills such as tips for Excel, guided form of meditation, presentation strategies, etc. When you provide a platform for all the people to exchange their knowledge, they will be benefitting from the professional form of development in the aspects of improved confidence, leadership, and also most importantly, improved creativity.

Encouraging Self-Reflection

As the workload tends to increase, it is very easy for every one of us to get focused on the work and just forget everything or the significance of what we all are actually accomplishing. Try to get all your team members to engage in the daily habit of self-reflection checking. This will be allowing us to reflect on all those things that we are actually achieving in life. It will also help in discovering all the connections that can help in inspiring or supporting the ongoing project.

Keeping a Schedule

It might really seem counter-intuitive for advocating more amount of free-thinking by simply creating a definite structure. But, keeping a proper schedule actually turns out to be really important for giving us time and the space for creating new things. In case you work from your home, you are having the benefit of scheduling flexibility by which you can keep the rest of your day for creativity and exercise. Even if you remain stuck for around eight to twelve hours every day, there are still various ways by which you can effectively break up the time that you have into several small chunks. This will allow you to manage your schedule properly. You need to block some specified times for some specific jobs. Try setting up an alarm in order to remind yourself of taking a break after long hours of work. When you take a break, just concentrate on thinking in a creative way. Try opening up your mind and dedicate all that time to find new things from all those things that already exist.

Learn Making Mistakes

Creativity is actually a very risky thing to do. When you start being creative, you will be pushing against all your boundaries. You are required to take the risk. You need to make more number of mistakes. Just allow yourself to make mistakes. If you just try to be perfect all the time, you are actually doing wrong. No one is perfect in this world. You will be learning from your own mistakes. In fact, mistakes can open up the doors to new prospects of creativity. If you try to operate from the safety boundary, you will be making your creativity suffer. Just try something new today. Risk it, fail in it, and try something else.

The best way of jumpstarting our creativity is by trying out something new. It does not mean that as you have been doing something in one way, it is the one and only way. Just put your thinking cap on and start listening to your gut for opting for projects or processes that no one has tried prior to you. Stand up from the office chair and start following the random hunch. It might turn out to be the most successful idea. And, if in case it does not turn out to be like that, just adjust the settings, adapt to it and try to make it even better the next time.

You can cultivate a culture in your workplace where your employees are encouraged to take risks. One of the primary reasons why your team members are not able to think outside the box or in a different way is because of their fear of failing and not getting support for their creativity. At every single turn, try to guide all your team members into learning the importance of a creative mind for business.

Providing Flexibility

Sometimes all that it needs for allowing the creative juices to flow is by bringing about some change in the scenery. In regular intervals, try to change the routine of your team members. Try venturing them outside the regular form of territory. Your team members will be able to think creatively outside their boundaries, where you will also have the mental makeup that you needed for your creativity. A flexible working policy can also help a lot in improving work productivity. Also, it can result in the development of brand new skills that will permit all your team members to bring in improved sense regarding the creativity of their minds. Additionally, you will be able to get the time to think something apart from your work.

Removing the Limits

In most of the large organizations, the leaders tend to invest huge amounts of money along with time for kicking off something new in the organization. But, what they also provide is a confined limit within which the other members need to get everything done. This can actually result in removing all forms of creativity from the workplace, especially when this thing happens from the side of a team leader. So, what are you supposed to do? You just need to provide the team with all that they require for getting everything done and just move out of their way. You will find new ideas and new strategies coming up on the board. Creativity is organic in nature and so it is not meant to be confined within a specified boundary.

Allowing Others to Test the Wings

We all need wings f0r flying in the sky of creativity and imagination. For learning how to fly, we are required to test the wings that we have got in the first place. This implies providing the chances of testing and trying out various things within the specified reasons. Just like any parent seeing their child fly for the very first time, some sort of guidance needs to be provided for avoiding any form of disaster. But, in actual, when it is in your workplace, you will either allow your team members to test out their very own creativity, or you will just be killing their creative drive by willing to contribute in their ideas. As the leader, you need to let them free and let them try out their creative aspects first.

Not Worrying About 'HOW'

Most of the leaders have the tendency of unknowingly weakening the creativity of their team simply by concentrating really early on the implementation. The fastest way in which a process of creativity can be killed is by asking your members for producing the tactical ways in which the ideas will be executed. This will not only by stifling the free flow of creative juice, but it will also be shifting the scenario of the working environment into a mindset of 'producing along with editing.' This ultimately results in reduced nature of contribution from each of the team members. Just stop thinking about HOW and allow the team members to first cultivate their creative ideas. This way you will be able to be creative as well with your team.

Offline Brainstorming

Among all the tools that are available for cultivating creativity, opting for offline brainstorming sessions is one of the best options. Try to encourage all the members of your team to come up with four to five unique creative ideas for any specific project. This will help in leveling the field of play both for the extroverts and the introverts. When each of the members generates a unique idea of their own, it will help in preventing individuals from bragging of their very own ideas that include the leader as well.

Building Up a Team of Diverse Nature

There are leaders who just have the tendency to hire some homogenous teams or hire by putting light on their very own image. What is better for encouraging creative acts within a team is to build the team in a way that contains various forms of strengths, skills, ideas and that can also encourage a healthy form of debate among all the members. Try to set up an environment where there is no form of shame if the members fail. The team needs to encourage different viewpoints for various ideas. You just need to omit the common expression, 'That is not how we work in here.'

Omitting BUT

Do not say 'but.' Whenever someone comes up with a new idea and you just speak up immediately by saying 'but'- whether it is 'but it is not possible for us' or 'but it is not within our budget' or 'but we do have enough finding,' what you are doing is preventing the creative juice from flowing freely. You are stopping the development of the ideas. Instead of 'but,' try saying 'and.' You are not required to agree all the time. There is no need of affirmation all the time. Just try saying 'yes, and' at the time of ideation and just try to observe what happens next. You just need to open up to a process of thinking which is free from the concept of failure.

Giving Out Direction

Innovation and creativity both need a balanced form of a hands-off approach. But, a proven killer of creativity is not giving out any form of direction. The teams of effective nature are required to be provided by a target on which they can aim. For obtaining an innovative and productive nature of solutions, try to provide the team with a basic goal along with some parameters. It is your duty to continuously check with the members of your team regarding what they require.

Being Gentle

The greatest issue that can effectively weaken creativity is not being gentle. It is not at all about how the ideas are being generated. It is only about the way in which the new ideas are being treated. In most of the cases, about 5% of the total ideas cannot be carried forward. But, the rest of the 95% ideas are required to be treated gently. When the ideas are treated with gentle care, it can help in keeping alive the creative aspect of all those who worked on them.

Being Curious

Nothing can better kill the aspect of creativity than a leader who omits risks and likes to play safe all the time. For sparking creativity, learn to be curious. You need to bring in the mind of a beginner to all the problems. You are required to channel your inner-self and learn to ask questions of appreciative nature, such as 'What are the possibilities on the other side?' Just try to listen to the answers from your inner-self and continue working on it the way your inner-self says.

CHAPTER 5
ENGAGING IN OBSERVATION SESSIONS

Creativity is very important for certain types of tasks in life. But, for aiding up that skill of creativity, you might need to get indulged in some sort of observation sessions. Tuning right into all those things that you can hear through the ears, the view that you can get with your eyes, the feelings of the same, and the energy that is possessed by the moment, each of these play a very important role in the complete process of creativity. Each of the elements can also influence the way how you are going to see each of the paths that are coming forward and also your willingness to take the very first step.

Practicing Balancing Observation Along With Actions

The skills of observation can function as a very powerful tool that can help in fine-tuning and playing each day. But, you are also required to feel when you are supposed to implement all those insights. Just sit and observe for a long time, and you will be able to psych out yourself. On the other aspect, taking some extra amount of time for thinking about the long and short benefits along with the risks can help in setting up a brand new process, a new client, or a new project that matches very well with all the desires and skills that you have got. When you decide of leaping in without any kind of research, emotional check or inner questioning, you might just be stepping into something that will be acting as a great distraction.

Also, jumping in without thinking much can help in inspiring you to make everything work with only all those things that you have got in hand. Neither of the two choices can turn out to be better than the other. They are actually a great example of the extremes, which can be served as a definite way of taking the skills of observation to a whole new level and also find out some creative and unique ways for applying them to the process of creativity.

Observation of good quality can actually bring you closer to all those things that you desire to create. It can also enlighten you with the reason behind your desire. It helps in lighting up the actual truth that lies around your authentic and unique voice. You can also learn how to use up what you hear, see, and feel for creating something from the core of your heart. As you improve your skills of observation actively, you will also be able to open up the doors to new pathways and ideas, while also offering yourself a path for releasing all the old judgments and patterns that cannot serve you any longer. Fine-tuning the skills of observation can actually go a very long way for understanding the meaning and the flow of your emotions and also for discovering various ways for maximizing the pockets of creative inspiration.

Seeing Everything As They Are

So, how did you actually do? To what limit were all your perceptions guided by the expectations? For being creative, you are required to dedicate yourself to view life as it is in the moment. This process actually begins with a real-time form of observation. We cannot actually give birth to observers simply by saying 'observe.' We are required to give ourselves the power along with means for this very observation. All such means can be procured by educating all our senses. Until and unless you can observe things in their authentic way, you will not be able to use them as authentic fuel for speeding up your creativity.

Six-Step Method

Observation is actually a slippery term. This is mainly because most of us think that as long as we tend to be conscious, we are actually observing. But, in actuality, it is not like that. For a true form of observation, let's have a look at the six-step method.

Intention

You need to be intentional while observing. What is defined by not being intentional is by saying, 'Today I will go to the mall and study people around me.' For making it really intentional, try adding a fixed time frame to it, for example, from 3 pm to 4 pm. Also, you will also need to set up various parameters such as you will be using a pen and paper for recording all that you observe. Observation will be losing its meaning without the proper intention.

Attention

Just leave back all your expectations at home. This is actually much easier to say than actually getting it done. Suppose you are sitting on a bench in a park and a couple is picnicking near you on a blanket. Suddenly, there is an argument between the two and the man tends to raise his voice for supporting his view. You start thinking that the guy will be able to defeat the woman on the argument by raising his voice. But, it could have happened exactly the opposite. You are required not to leave any space for your expectations. Do not just try to approach any person, bush, or mountain with your expectations of 'personness,' 'bushness, or 'mountainness.' Instead of doing that, just permit the uniqueness of each of them to immerge just like that you haven't ever seen them prior in your life.

Focus

Start filtering out all those things that are not actually worthy or subject of your own attention. This might turn out to be difficult as every one of us has the habit of using our imagination along with our expectations while the surrounding controls all our senses. Focus is like a habit that can be developed simply by learning to recognize and then followed by not paying attention to the stimuli of attention with a mindset of 'not right now.'

Notation

Start briefing all the observations that are unrefined within your notebook. Just relax and opt for following the guide of your inner-self. Start making the notations but only to that extent for reminding your mind at a later stage for the insights.

Transfer

After you are done with your schedule of the observation period, start transferring all the raw notes that you have taken in your smaller notebook into a large-sized notebook. Start refining all of them, try to re-imagine them, and write down everything freshly in the large notebook. Anything that you have left on the pocket notebook and that has not been refined or transferred on that day only, have high chances of turning into a wasted effort.

Application

As soon as you are done with the task of transferring, start applying all the new forms of acquisitions that you have observed into a creative setting. You can apply them to any situation, character, or even a new project.

Describing Everything Felt and Perceived

Set your timer to 10 minutes. Now, you are required to again back in your imagination to the scene of observation and start describing in your notebook all that you have heard, saw, tasted, smelled, and felt. Try to be as specific as you can. Make sure that you have highlighted each and every aspect of your observation scene. After the timer is up, just put down the pen and take a break for a few minutes. After the break is over, start the timer again and repeat the process for the scenes that you haven't described yet.

How to Choose an Observation Spot?

Well, any type of place can turn out to be your spot of observation. But, if you still want something definite for definite creativity, follow these tips.

- **Choosing a scheduled spot:** It can be a meadow, a park, a country road, or a beach with the shoreline in front of you. In short, you can choose any place that is calm and inspiring in nature. Try choosing a place where no one can distract you. It can also help in improving your concentration and focus.

- **Choosing a spot that is permanent:** When talking about a permanent spot, what I mean is that lookout for spots that will be the same after five minutes or five days from now. It will help you in going back to the place again and again whenever you need to spark your creativity.

- **Establishing a reference frame:** It cannot be excessively small but it can actually be very large. When you are at the beach, the reference frame might turn out to be as small just like a seashell but it should not be larger than what your eyes can actually see without moving your head. If there is any kind of negative view within your frame, try omitting it when you use it as your reference.

CHAPTER 6
HOW CAN SOCIALIZING OUTSIDE THE NORMAL CIRCLES HELP?

In the new economy of today, knowledge is often considered to be the key factor that can help in achieving as well as sustaining the organizational form of competitive advantage. Socialization is, most of the time, considered as being very important and also a beneficial process for creating values. But, in actual practice, it gets overshadowed by storage and capturing of knowledge which is largely driven by the advancements in information technology. For long term success for an organization, creativity and socialization are the key forms of drivers. When you deliberately move for enabling the creative aspect and by turning the innovative nature of behavior of everyone into something special, you can give birth to a whole new idea.

Socialization and the Stops

Socialization comes along with a component in the process of creativity. That very component is the 'stop.' Creativity goes through phases of breaks, deep immersion, pauses, and frustration until it reaches a stopping point. At that very point, the social component comes into play. There are two types of stopping points.

- **Creative block stop:** In this aspect, you have already exhausted the free flow of creativity, and now you are in dire need of some form of detachment in order to continue with the overall process. You just need a way that can effectively help in rekindling the fire. Socializing our work that has been done is a great way of achieving more than one form of detachment and it might even take various forms. It can be like gathering valuable feedbacks, discussing the latest form of developments with any individual, or just simply observing what is being done by others. It is also very much useful to socialize with fellow creative individuals because the positive effect of networking for the ideas can trigger a brand new work phase all alone.

- **Good enough stop:** When there are no forms of internal blocks, there might be moments when you recognize that the job that has been done by you has much more than enough shape and is now complete for sharing with other individuals. This is actually the revision phase, where looking out for honest feedback and advice actually provides a positive nature of boost for the working process.

As you develop your very own creativity, it is actually important for recognizing these sorts of stops as soon as you can. It will help you in planning the correct strategy for future progress and also with a much higher degree of self-satisfaction. This component of socialization is also very important when it comes to group creativity. Even in large groups, discussing, socializing, and sharing ideas is an important element. Socialization helps in mingling the mindsets of various types of people that finally gives birth to a new form of an idea. In fact, it has been found that all those ideas that evolved from socialization are the most unique ones in structure, and the success rate of such ideas also tends to be higher than others.

How to Socialize Even If You Are an Introvert?

If you are the kind of person who is sort of private in nature or rather an introvert, you actually know the pain that you need to face in any party, meetings, or networking events. You prefer to stay at home for staying away from such situations and try to be creative and innovative on your own by reading books, listening to music, and by remaining introspective. But, you might not have any idea that not socializing enough can hamper your creative aspect. Even though if you socialize within your known circle, it is not going to help you in any way. You might feel tensed or disturbed whenever you try to meet new people or start a conversation with unknown people.

As an introvert, you might generally: 1) Feel comfy on your own 2) Like to know only a limited number of people 3) Like to be reserved. Well, it is a common thing that happens with the introverts, and all that you need to do is to follow all these tips.

Going Out When You Are Not Willing to

If you do not like socializing much, it might actually feel a bit tempting to reject all the invitations that you receive. You can actually keep on doing this for the rest of your life. But, in actuality, it is not at all a healthy practice. You are unknowingly suppressing all the new ideas along with your creative aspects. If you are feeling demotivated, socializing can help in bringing in the required motivation that can help you to get started with your new work. This is because, as you meet new people, everyone comes with a different mindset of their own. You will have exposure to various types of ideas and feedbacks that can give birth to a new idea.

Connecting With the Connectors

One of the great ways of expanding your social boundary is by connecting to that individual who can help you in meeting with others. These 'connector' types of people are the ones who are social media addicts, love to host new parties, and are most of the time seen with a huge group of people around them. Such individuals are actually very open by nature and you can connect with them very easily. Although they might not have enough time to invest in a deep nature of friendship with you, they would love to add more people to their social circle from which you can get to know more people as well.

Continuously Meeting New People

It is a great habit when you keep on meeting new people whom you can add to your social circle. In actuality, all the people that you are going to meet will not turn out to be your friends, and not all the friends that you are having now will be around you forever. That is why it is always said that if you are not into the act of making new friends, you are making fewer in actual. You are always recommended to go to new types of places where you can find it easy to walk up to and also introduce yourself to some new individuals. Ideally, you should be going to all those places where other people are also open for meeting new individuals such as opening nights, trade shows, seminars, talks, charity or cultural events.

Establishing Your Image As a Value Giver

While you are on the go to meet brand new people, you are required to hook. Nothing can actually hook better than having an attitude of a giver. First, you need to listen to them and start imagining as if you were that individual or individuals and start seeing the world from their eyes. Second, you need to be willing to share some contacts, stories, or even a piece of quick advice on the subject they are discussing or talking about. As you meet new people, some psychological principles work in the background that can easily determine whether they are going to meet you again in the future or not. This actually functions on a level of unconsciousness. The best principle is adopting the taker or giver attitude. If they are going to sense that what you only care about is about yourself, the connection is not going to take place.

But, how to portray the attitude of a giver? You just need to need to pay close attention to them, their stories or attitude, and start talking in the aspect that interests them.

Start Paraphrasing

If you are an introvert by nature, you might often experience a social form of anxiety. In such situations, you are most likely to find yourself having a blank talk in the middle of a conversation with others. But, there is nothing to freak out in actual. Whenever you find that you are actually drawing a blank nature of mid-convo, just try to paraphrase. It can help you in bringing the conversation or chat back on the track.

Knowing the Type of Friends You Actually Desire in Advance

Right before you start investing all your time in making brand new friends, start it off with a little bit of planning. First, try to figure out your own character and the type of people you like or that can match you. You can list out some qualities, interests or traits of characters that you would like in your new friends. There is nothing to hesitate in being a little ambitious than you usually do. This is actually very important as it will be allowing your mind to judge quickly whether the person that you just met is a good fit for your life or not.

You can start with some definite qualities such as interesting, giver, funny, honest, ambitious, curious, loyal, and reliable. You can freely add more qualities if you want. Such a list of qualities can provide you with the clarity that you need for making new friends. It will also be saving a lot of your time, along with frustration.

CHAPTER 7
IDEAS AND BOOKS

Most of us do not just sit down and start reading a novel because we want to develop some new ideas and improve our imagination and thus be more creative by nature, do we? The majority of us love to read as we want to escape the world. As we read, we get into the mind of the writer and his own world and start living a completely different sort of life, but only for a short period of time. We always try to get entertained by the imaginary world that is being created by the writer along with the characters that populate in that very world. But, what actually makes us stick to the book and the story that the writer has written? This is mainly because the writer has easily managed to engage all out senses of imagination. In simple terms, reading has the power of stimulating our imagination to create a whole new world inside our minds.

Reading and Creativity

If you were a real explorer, you would have learned the various aspects of the world along with its diversity by directly experiencing them. You would have been walking down narrow roads in some foreign country, sail your boat on the great seas, sip tea in any courtyard of the Middle East or hop around on the sand dunes of the great deserts. This very exploration could help in broadening up your mind, develop your very own imagination, change your perception of the world, and boost up your creativity. If you are capable of seeing all the places imagining what exactly it would feel like, you are actually working on your imagination. But, we cannot take up the high roads and just disappear within the sunset of the horizon most of the time for having all these experiences.

But, what we can do is to read books and discover the new worlds, the world which is unknown to us. As you read a book, it starts using up your imagination, and this results in the development of your creativity. Obviously, the primary key for developing the required amount of imagination while reading any book is actually the interest level that you have right in the book content. The more you get absorbed in any book, the more it will be able to stimulate all your imagination and thus, help improve your creativity. In fact, as you keep on reading, it can actually improve your knowledge bank which is really important for giving birth to new ideas.

Books come along with different types of ideas or plots that can help in taking you to a similar situation in your mind. From that very situation, what you can gain is the idea of a new plan of action. You just need to concentrate your mind on what you read, and no extra form of effort is required to cultivating a new idea or plan. So, it can be said that reading books can actually improve our creative aspect of mind.

Reading and Brain Functioning

For improving the aspect of your creativity, having proper brain functioning is of utmost importance. As we keep on reading books, we get the best benefits of creativity from the writing when we start using our power of imagination for interpreting what we are reading. It has been found from various studies that reading can help in boosting mental creativity and capacity. Also, it can help in improving our brain function. It enhances the connectivity of the brain. Reading is often regarded as the exercise for our minds. It might sound cliché, but it is actually true. Mental fitness is very important besides physical fitness, especially when it comes to the aspect of ideas and creativity.

When you read for only about half an hour every day, it can flex the muscles of your mind. It can help you in thinking, fantasizing, and use up your imagination.

Reading and Better Concentration

We are all living in the age of information. A really fast-paced world where all of us are getting surrounded with gadgets bombarding us with links, data, words, ads, updates, and other types of information that is actually problematic for all of us to digest and process. It might actually be a very overwhelming situation, but it has got a very simple solution. Just turn off your mobile, TV or computer and pick a book. Try to concentrate on everything you read. Television is actually noisy and passive in nature. But, books need active concentration along with engagement. They can absorb our minds completely. It takes lots of effort to read the words, finding out the meaning, and understanding why were they written like this.

As you read, you are building up images, opinions, and thoughts in your mind. You are putting into use your power of critical thinking along with proper logic for processing the information for properly understanding the concepts and the ideas that are being conveyed by the author. The more we can train our brain for concentrating, the easier it is going to be. Reading can readily improve your concentration and that ultimately results in a clear form of thinking which is very important when it comes to creativity and new ideas.

Reading and Knowledge Base

The more you are going to read, the more number of things you will come to know and the more you learn, the more places you can go to. Reading can trigger lifelong learning and also an insatiable thirst for gaining knowledge. Books are often regarded as the window to the wide world outside- a small glimpse of the cultural past, the present, and the future, as it is being interpreted by the writer and filtered by the mesh of our imaginations. As you keep on reading, you can discover a great amount of information regarding where you have been, where you are going, and also how everything around you works. The more you come to know, the more you can share with your mind. You can also turn out to be a great starter of conversations, a great solver of problems, and also a very quick thinker.

No matter what sort of career field you are opting for or you are already into, all of these skills can help you a lot in your journey. Just turn off everything around you and dedicate only 30 minutes every day for your brain when you will be reading books. Try to notice how much better you can feel. You will actually be surprised by seeing the results.

Reading and Boosting of Confidence

As you read, you will be ending up with a large stock of vocabulary. It will be increasing exponentially as you keep on reading. Words can nurture your creativity. When you have lots of words at your disposal, you can turn out to be a great communicator. As you learn to communicate with others about your ideas, you will be establishing confidence in your ideas. And, when you have proper confidence in your ideas, you can now explore your world of imagination.

How to Be Creative By Reading Books?

First, let us just jot down all those things that actually make an individual creative. The primary thing that comes into play is the power of imagination, then comes the capability of breaking the boundaries of thinking followed by continuous learning of new things, and last but not least, experiences for evolving new ideas. Reading can help a lot in improving the powers of innovation and creativity. Let's find out how it is done.

- **Enhances your imagination:** By remaining stuck in our usual thread of life, we will never be able to gather the sort of awareness that actually feeds the skills of our imagination. Reading can help in creating a completely different world for us and also permits us to reign in that world according to our imagination. The door to the world, which was unimagined opens up while reading. For example, Harry Potter which was created by J.K. Rowling created a new world where we are able to find ourselves in that world, doing certain actions that we desire to. In the world of imagination, there is no form of boundary and thus, it can allow us to collect new ideas from that very world.

- **Widens up the boundaries of thinking:** While sitting in a busy café in New York City, will you be able to describe a quiet and soothing hill destination? Having the ability to think about various scenarios and also describing them fluently needs lots of knowledge along with awareness. Reading is often regarded as the best tool for doing so. It not only lends wisdom but it also opens up our minds to various forms of possibilities along with the vastness of the world. You can break free and start thinking on your own. As you start thinking freely, you will also be able to give birth to new ideas or provide the existing ideas with the missing parts.

- **Language:** As you read, you can have phrased words that are designed beautifully, new meanings, and inspiring quotes right in the grip of your hand. Literature in the most basic form is nothing but several words sewed together in a special way in order to convey an interesting story. Words can provide us with the inspiration that we need to boost up our creativity and expand our world of imagination. Also, as you come across beautiful quotes while reading, it can provide you with the required amount of motivation as well.

- **Allows us to learn in a consistent way:** In general, our action of earning tends to stop as we complete our education. But beyond that, we need to make certain efforts to expose ourselves to the light of knowledge. Reading is the only habit that can provide us with learning as each and every step. Creativity, in general, has a lot to do with the extent of your knowledge and how learned you are. It is also concerned about how open you are for new contexts and perspectives in life.

- **Substitute experiencing:** The more we experience, the more we will be able to imagine, and thus, the more we will be capable of creating. But, while speaking truly, keeping an account of all your personal experiences can actually limit the extent of your creativity. While you read, it is somewhat like living several lives at once. It can easily make up for all those things that you have not been capable of experiencing in your life.

- **A new life lens:** While reading, your focus will move from yourself, your issues, and your struggles. You will get the chance of peering into the life and psyche of another individual and just see how they are finding solutions to all their problems. You will be getting a new life lens with which you can have a look at your own life.

- **Allows your creative juice to flow:** Everyone loves to read a good book. As you start reading a good book or novel, you are actually allowing your creative juices to flow freely. You can learn from the life experiences of the character in the book. But, as you re-read the book again, you can have the chance to use your newly acquired life experiences and learn from the characters again. You can shape the experiences that you get and also interpret the theme of creativity. Creativity is all about letting the imagination flow freely and that is what reading provides us with.

- **It is a powerful part of what is created by you:** Whether you are building, writing, cooking, painting- whatever you do that needs your creativity, unfolds some of the stories that you are actually living. When you read the stories of others, it can effectively fill up your mind with more number of problems that require solutions, ideas that are waiting for exposure, and beauty that needs to be shared. What you read also consists of a part of your life, from your own eyes.

CHAPTER 8

SPEAKING OUT THE IDEAS

Here is a very common scenario that most of us are familiar with: You have just come up with a great idea which you think that all of your colleagues, along with the organization, can benefit from. But, even after thinking that the idea is full proof and solid, you are still very afraid of speaking up loud about the idea that you have in your mind. You know that it will actually be smart of you if you speak up about the same, but how are others going to react to it? And, even the worse, what if others think that the complete is actually very dumb? In all such cases, we just end up in keeping shut and then just see someone else raising their hands and coming up with a similar kind of idea in front of others and getting the praises. Well, this should not be the case. When you are confident about your idea and you know that it is actually going to work, at least from your own perspective, there is nothing wrong with speaking up about the same.

It is actually okay to fail or when others think that your idea is dumb. You are never going to get feedback about your idea unless and until you can speak up about it. And, until you get feedback, you cannot actually start working on it or improvise the same. So, in order to get all your ideas into work, learn to come up in the front and speak up.

Half-Baked Ideas Can Help in Starting Beneficial Conversations

If you are having any half-baked sort of idea which you are not confident about to speak up, it can help in starting important conversations. Most of us think that we can only speak up when we have some sort of idea that is complete in nature. But, in actual, speaking about even about the half-baked ideas can help in adding in the required features that were missing earlier. You can have the scope of modifying the future aspects of the idea and work on it with others. You can also include others in that very idea by talking about the same in front of others. The best part about it is that you can get some beneficial advice from your team members.

Unless You Speak Up, No One Is Going to Speak for You

Well, it is actually very frustrating when a member of your team comes up with an idea that is similar to yours or is similar to something that you were recently thinking about. Although it is not guaranteed all the time that someone else will surely come up with a similar sort of idea. In case you have full-on inspiration about any idea and you have something that you feel like talking about, it is completely up to you whether or not you will be speaking up. Keeping aside the worst-case scenario where someone else is getting all the credits for a similar kind of idea, what is even worse is that you might be keeping to yourself an idea that can change the world. When you keep your mouth shut by not speaking up, you are actually providing your organization with a disservice. Also, unless and until you speak up, nobody will be speaking up for you in your support of the idea.

How to Get the Confidence for Speaking Up?

Many of us have the phobia of speaking confidently about our ideas in front of others. But, this very phobia is not at all healthy when you want to grow and bring about a change, especially in the world of business. You have inputs, questions, and ideas- various things that are required to be addressed for running the project smoothly. However, the fear of failure and shame can easily prevent you from opening up and thus resulting in zero processing of your idea. As you learn to speak up at the time of office conversations or meetings, it will not only help you in being engaged with all your peers but it will also be helping you to solve various problems. Here are certain tips that you can follow to get the confidence that you need to speak up.

Taking Tiny Steps Before the Big Run

When you are having a fear of voicing up about any idea of yours, try to share the idea first and also ask for feedback from any individual whom you trust completely. When you are done with this, commit yourself to share one single comment at the time of meeting to introduce your idea. After that, try inviting some perspectives from outside by asking some of the witnesses what that they actually feel about your idea or contribution. As you get some sort of credible feedback from any trusted nature of source, it can easily boost up your confidence level and thus help you in finding your lost voice.

Finding Out Occasions When You Feel Like Speaking

Try asking yourself if there has been any particular occasion where you did not have difficulty in speaking up and expressing your views. This could also be an occasion that is outside your work boundary, with family and friends. As you have identified that very occasion, now ask yourself what was the thing that you were doing in a different way. You can also opt for another approach by imagining yourself in a situation one year back when you were confident and direct. What was the thing that you did differently?

Developing the Skills In Environments of Lower Risk

Start identifying some of the opportunities for getting out of the comfort zone. Try looking out for environments or even people that come with lower risk or where you can have a support system of strong nature for trying out new things. Let any trusted mentor or colleague of yours know that you are willing to build up confidence in this particular area and ask them for observing and sharing their feedback for helping you to help in growing. Just like any type of skill, the practice can easily help you in improving.

Writing Down Everything That You Will Be Saying

As you write down all those things that you are going to say, it can help a lot in dealing with all your struggles of speaking up and minimizes all your stumbles. You need to remember that it is absolutely okay to read out all your feelings and thoughts. It will be coming out of your head and will turn out to be much clear and concise. It will allow others to find out how important it is to you and all the efforts that you have put in it. You can speak up much easier by writing down all the things.

Defining Why The Voice Is So Important

The small nature of voices can have a big impact. Try starting a conversation with your very own self. Why are all those things that you are going to say taking over your nerves? How are you going to help by raising up your voice? Why will your words be welcome in this world? As you start gaining confidence in all your why start making up space for other individuals by asking them what exactly is important for them. You need to start out small and keep on practicing daily.

Taking the Required Action in Place of Just Looking Out for Perfection

Many of us tend to struggle with this issue. The primary mistake that is made by the majority of the people is that they start believing they need to feel super confident for acting with confidence. Well, in reality, it is the reverse. Confidence can be acquired by taking the necessary actions. As you start doing the thing, you will automatically get the power. Just stop waiting till the time your idea or you are completely ready. You need to create your own confidence by speaking up and taking action.

Acting After Visualizing the Conversation

Instead of just diving in and taking the steps carefully, begin by first visualizing the conversation or meeting. Try watching the whole room nod in accordance with your idea as you competently and confidently start articulating your own view. You can easily witness the overall shift in your mind as you start rehearsing the outcome. Right after you are done with the task of visualization, try converting it into a reality. As you step out and be brave, you are actually giving yourself access to grow.

Focusing on the Facts and Not on Emotions

For allowing others to properly align with all your opinions, solutions, and suggestions, you need to be absolutely clear about how you are going to communicate them. You will be able to boost up your confidence as you start sharing the facts and stats and not trying to be emotional about what you want to share. You can have greater strength as you start speaking up with clear nature of the conviction.

Paying Proper Attention to the Verbal and Body Language

Your verbal language, as well as your body language work hand in hand. When you have proper body language coupled with the right verbal language, you can just blow everyone's mind. You will tend to feel more confident about anything you speak. Also, it can allow you to leave a lasting impression on others as you speak. For improving your body and verbal language, you can start by videotaping yourself and then rectify all the mistakes or improve what is needed.

Getting Rid of the Outcomes

One of the primary things that prohibit people from speaking up and sharing their own opinions is that they are concerned about the outcomes of what they share. If you just let go of all the perceived outcomes and just start sharing because you want to share and voice up, you will learn to be less concerned about what others do or think in response to your action. Just start speaking up and fully express your very own position. Do not think about the response, and it will turn out to be worth the action.

Being an Advocate for Other People

You can be the advocate of other people who are facing some tough time in getting their voice out and speak up for their opinions. Try searching for that person who keeps on raising his/her hand and gets overlooked all the time. Try helping others when they want to speak up or say something. You will tend to feel empowered as you will jump in with your personal thoughts. It will also provide you with the confidence that you need to speak up your own thoughts and ideas.

Waiting for a Better Opportunity

The effective listeners are equally important besides the noisy members of a meeting who always keeps the room filled with their importance and voice. Try to listen to them and watch their behavioral patterns along with the style of speaking. You can easily find the perfect spot for yourself to speak up when you keep on tracking them. Always remember that sometimes the only way of being heard in a large meeting is right after the meeting when your competitor speakers are respected and appreciated for their thoughtful and reflective style.

CHAPTER 9
VISUALIZATION OF IDEAS

When you hear the very common phrase 'Start visualizing your life, your goals, your success,' probably it is not going to be the first time that you actually hear it. Each and every time when you achieve something in our life, your mind plays a big role in it. Ideas and goals are parts of our lives. They can actually be as small as 'I will be exercising daily from today' or really big like 'I will be starting my very own company by the next two months.' They are very effective in giving our life a purpose and also a guiding idea for our daily lives. Right after that comes in the funny part- realization. It actually takes in a lot of hard work along with dedication and determination to keep your head right in the direction of success. But, what will happen if you get stuck and are unable to move further for setting your idea or goal?

In most of the cases, people tend to get stuck because of their fear, the fear of failure, and social pressure. And, that is when the superpower of visualization comes to play. It comes along with a key feature- the projection of a simple mental image of the future days that is going to be the present one day.

How Does Visualization Actually Work?

Whether you are a student, businessman, or an entrepreneur, visualization can be applied at any point of your life. As you start using it, you will be able to picture and also feel the success right in your mind, much before you will do in reality. The more detailed you can visualize all your ideas, the higher will be the chances of you working on it and getting success. By that, it is not only meant about the absolute end results but also the sacrifices and barriers that are going to come in the way. Try picturing how you will be feeling and what will be your next plan right after you have achieved your goal.

The key to visualization is simple; the more real and vivid you can get, the stronger the effect is going to be. Have you ever come across or heard about an entrepreneur who is actually successful now and did not believe his vision and himself? No one can actually find a successful entrepreneur of this sort. If you are not going to have full faith in what you are visualizing, there are high chances that you will not be able to achieve the goals.

Visualizing a Favorable Future

It is very easy to focus on all those things that are wrong in life instead of trying to look out for a better future as all your problems are actually real. Visualization without any form of action is futile in nature as inspired actions, and mental preparations are both important for bringing your desires to life. Visualization is nothing more than the seed that is fertilized in your mind, where taking actions is like a flowering plant that actually blossoms. One needs another for manifesting all your dreams and goals. No one can assure that a new idea will be able to change the course of your life. But, as you visualize, you can get a signal whether or not the idea is going to work out.

It is extremely beneficial to visualize your favorite form of future in place of just thinking about all the circumstances that annoy you daily. Most people have the tendency to act in an impulsive way without thinking about what they actually want in life. They keep on thinking about what they do not want in life and get disheartened after it shows up as something different than expected. This is mainly because they failed to devote enough energy and time to get clear notions about their ideas and desires. The attitude of your mind is actually important as it can effectively convert your brain into an electromagnet that can attract the opposite side of your dominating thoughts, purposes, and aims. It can also attract the counterpart of your worries, doubts, and fears.

Nourishing the Mind With Proper Impression

The neurons that are fired together can wire together. The cells of your brain that contact frequently can be strengthened with their very own connection. All the messages that are traveling on the same path of the brain tend to become more efficient and faster. This is actually very important for various reasons. As you keep on giving all your attention to all those things that you do not want in your life, the same structures of the cells tend to get strengthened and thus become more efficient until and unless there is a change in the pattern of your thoughts. During certain times of the day such as early in the morning or late in the evening, visualization tends to be more conducive as your mind is less agitated at that moment.

Try thinking of these time periods as the opportunity windows for bathing your thoughts and mind with ideas and images for creating the ideal form of your future. The correct time in the day can help in properly nourishing our minds, along with the perfect impressions. While an amount of visualization is important, you also need to remember that you are actually dealing with a form of power that is similar to the ground soil, which can only produce the desired plant when the seed is planted by you. Your thoughts are like seeds and your mind is the ground soil. We always keep on planting, followed by harvesting. All that you are required to do is to plant only that seed which you actually want to grow and harvest.

Forming a Mental Picture of the Ideal Future

Imagination is often regarded as the beginning of new creation. You will imagine all those things that you desire, you will do what you imagine, and you will also create what you imagined. Imagination can act as a great power that can provide human beings with the capability of creating their own future. But, in order to get the best out of it, you can are required to devote consistent effort along with time for developing the powers of your mind so that it turns out to be laser-focused. Visualization needs patience, time, and diligence. Prayer is also a form of visualization and so are your words, and so it makes complete sense in using your powers of creativity for visualizing your future.

You need to avoid yourself from attention to all those things with which you are not at all happy in life. Try not to write or talk about the same. Just focus on that thing that you want to build up by devoting five minutes daily for visualizing the same. We are not capable of choosing our very own circumstances, but what we can choose is our thoughts and thus indirectly takes part in shaping the circumstances. Many of the great thinkers used to daydream just for enhancing their abilities of creativity. What they did is to just sit in any comfortable place and permitted their minds to wander off on their own.

Whatever you want to bring to life needs to be cultivated and visualized in the first place in your mind until it tends to feel like real. We often come to hear in our lives that we only use 10% of our mental capacity. This is mainly because we haven't yet developed the theory of creating our lives with the help of our thoughts. Try taking a consistent form of action for supporting all that you visualize. Always remember that the right action and visualization work in harmony with each other.

Techniques of Visualization

There are various techniques that can be used for shining the light of visualization on your future life. Let's have a look at them.

Treasure Map

This technique of visualization uses up both the components- physical and mental. But, I do not actually mean an actual treasure map along with the mentality of a pirate.

First, imagine yourself obtaining a treasure and then start sketching out all the physical forms of representation of each and every component that is involved. You can draw a ship, a rough landscape for representing a proper path and also a cool island in order to indicate the location. You need to understand that in this technique, the drawings are not that much important when compared to the visualization of the same. Your mind will be projecting a road right to the goal where the spot is marked by X. As it can easily be assumed that this technique needs a lot of patience along with lack of distractions, so it is better to find a place first where you can have all of these ideal conditions.

Receptive Visualization

This technique is actually a bit passive when compared with the technique of a treasure map. It also needs a serene nature of the surroundings. The best way in which this technique can be described is by assuming you are the director of a movie. You have the power to control all the scenes of your movie. As you are clear with the image, start adding components that will make the image feel more dynamic and lively in nature until you come to feel that you are the only one who is a part of both decision making and the required actions.

Altered Memory

Try to be truthful, how many times in your life a specific event turned out to be in a less favorable way for you just wishing to change or alter it? Well, this technique uses up this very thing as the driving force. All that you need to do is to replay all the scenes in your mind while also replacing or altering all the negative responses along with situations with controlled and positive ones. It might feel a lot difficult as you start with it, but trust me, once you are successful in recreating the scenes and altering them, the uncomforting feeling, along with the memories of the real event, will be fading away eventually. You just need to keep on practicing.

Goal Pictures

This is often regarded as a very powerful technique of visualization. The aim is to create pictures of yourself along with your idea or goal. Try picturing it as if it has been completed and achieved. If your goal is to start a new office, try collecting a picture of an office from the internet and cut out a picture of yourself and paste it on the same. The main idea is to visualize yourself with the goal of your life. This will help you in fighting for it daily until and unless you have achieved it in real life.

Index Cards

Every one of us has a long list of ideas and goals, about 30 or 40, that we all are currently working on. The main aim is to take small index cards and write one of our goals in each of the cards. Try keeping the same near your bed as you sleep and take the stack of cards with you as you travel. You need to go through the stack of cards at least once in a day, where you will be picking up only one card at once. Read the card and close your eyes, try seeing the goal as being completed and the result as you want.

CHAPTER 10
BREAKING THE PATTERN FOR NEW IDEAS

Having a solid form of daily routine can definitely benefit our private life as well as our work. Not only you will be able to check out things from your to-do list, but you can also reduce your stress level, improve the condition of your mental health, and break the bad habits. But, as you tend to get settled within a fixed form of routine, your brain will start functioning on autopilot. It will be suppressing all the interesting and exciting information from the world outside your mind. This will result in you stopping to search out for new ideas. You will tend to restrict yourself from working only with a limited quantity of information.

Breaking routines at regular intervals is actually a great form of challenge for the brain. It needs to re-evaluate what exactly is happening and will thus start to operate with increased ability. As you break your daily routine once, you will come to see the world from a completely different angle. When you perceive the environment with your fresh eyes, it can permit the possibility of questioning what you are basing your thoughts on. This will ultimately allow you to think in a different way, and you will also be able to develop new ideas that you haven't thought about before.

You are required to go to places for meeting creative people and take in all their inspiring ideas. Your ideas are somewhat like networks. All that they consist of are thoughts that have been recently connected. So, if you are willing to develop some brilliant ideas, all that you need to do is to develop some fresh new thoughts followed by connecting them with a great network. Breaking your daily routines and opting for some chaotic environment can help you a lot in doing so.

Techniques of Breaking the Pattern

Every one of us has the tendency to get stuck in certain patterns of thinking. As you break all of these patterns, you can easily free up your mind and start with the creation of new ideas. Here are some techniques that you can follow for cracking up the patterns of thinking.

Challenging Assumptions

Try challenging all your assumptions and start rethinking the perceptions, from a completely different view. No matter what is the situation that you need to face, you are only holding on to a predefined set of assumptions. As you challenge all of these assumptions, you can easily broaden the awareness of the new possibilities that you haven't come across before in your life. You can start by asking out 'why' and just keep on drilling down, asking why repeatedly for every answer. When you use this approach, you will be able to find out some new form of insights about your ideas.

Rephrasing the Problem

Try rephrasing the problem that you are having; look at it from a different angle. As you keep on expressing the problems in different ways, you might often find out the way to new ideas. For rewording of the problem that you are facing, see it from a different perspective, 'What is the need for solving this very problem?' , 'What are the obstacles and challenges that I need to overcome for solving this problem?' As you ask this nature of questions, you can easily gain a greater insight into the problem. When you solve new problems, you can generate new ideas from the initial root of the problem. In fact, problems are often regarded as the storehouse of new ideas. The more problems you can deal with in your life, the more will be the chance of you getting new ideas.

Provoke

Try provoking all the thoughts that you are having and take them to the extremes. Reverse the ordinary form of conventions or try to bring up the radical nature of alternatives. If you think that you are unable to come up with something new, you can try things by turning them upside-down. In place of just thinking about and focusing on problem-solving or boosting up the development of a product, try to find out the ways in which you could have created the problem or have impaired the development of the product. You will actually be surprised after finding out the number of reverse ideas that you can come up with. You need to learn to regard all of these new thoughts after you have successfully reversed them once more, use them as a feasible solution for the original issues.

Expressing By Using an Alternative Media

You can start expressing yourself and your thoughts via a different form of media and find out some new possibilities for shaping your idea. Everybody in this world comes with multiple intelligences in place of only one general nature of intelligence. When we face some complex sort of challenge, we try to express our thoughts by solely using our ability of verbal reasoning. Next time when you face a complex challenge, try to use a different sort of media in order to communicate all your thoughts. Try being creative; there are several ways of expressing the issue. For instance, you can use toy blocks, clay, paint, word associations, or music.

But, remember, do not try to solve the problem or issue right in this phase. Just keep on expressing it and have fun as you discover new tools. Your brain will keep on working on the initial issue or problem unconsciously, trying its best to process the very information in a different way. While doing so, it can also trigger new patterns of thinking, which can ultimately result in the generation of creative ideas.

Breaking the pattern can actually be fun. The way you do it will determine whether you will be enjoying it or not. Instead of doing things in a conventional way, try doing them in a way that you haven't done before. What you will be receiving are some new ideas along with the fun and joy of doing something different. In fact, when you try to lead your mind and thinking process on a predefined path, there are high chances that your life will tend to be monotonous, without having the ability to come up with some new sort of idea. You have got all that you need. You just have to use them properly for shaping your life the way you want.

CONCLUSION

Thank you for making it through to the end of *The Great Ideas Generator: Unleash Your Inner Potential, Learn How To Use Your Brain More Effectively* let's hope it was informative and able to provide you with all of the tools you need to achieve your goals whatever they may be.

Now, your only job is to start developing new ideas with all the tips and techniques that you have learned from this book. Ideas can change your life. But, if you are thinking of keeping them suppressed right within your mind, you will be suppressing your life in actuality. Why keep something secret that might have the potential of changing the whole world? Try visualizing all the ideas that you have got in your mind and think of them as being completed. You can easily gain an insight into whether you should keep on working on it or not. Also, if you are still thinking in the way that you generally use to, it is high time now that you change that habit. In order to do something different, you need to think differently as well.

The best thing that you can do is share your ideas with others and keep track of the feedback that you receive. This will help you to make the necessary changes that you need to make in your idea for making it full proof.

Finally, if you found this book useful in any way, I would be happy if you leave me an objective review along with a review on Amazon.

DESCRIPTION

Buy the Paperback Version of this Book and get the Kindle eBook version absolutely for FREE!

If you really want to give birth to some new ideas and also turn them into reality, keep on reading.

Well, you must have come across several books that talk about the generation of ideas. You might also have attended some mind-blowing seminar of talk shows hosted by a really successful person, who is willing to share some of his ideas with you so that you can also do the same. But, have you really been able to gain something from them? Were you able to generate something which you can call it your very own? No, right? Do you know the reason behind this? This is mainly because most of the books that you have read told you only about the ideas that you need to opt for. Most of the talk shows told you only about the ideas that the speaker generated. If you are looking out for the basics and want to learn how to generate ideas, you can take help from this book *The Great Ideas Generator: Unleash Your Inner Potential, Learn How To Use Your Brain More Effectively*. You will come to know about the various aspects of idea generation along with the basics of creating your own idea. This book is capable of showing you the right path.

Here is a summarized format of all the main elements which you can find in this book

- Innovation and creativity work hand in hand. Both depend on each other. Also, if you cannot establish these two aspects of your life and everything that you do, new ideas cannot be generated.

- We all are creative in our own ways. But, have you ever thought about why creativity tends to decrease as we grow up? The answer to this question is very simple. You just need to keep alive your childish creative mind for the best possible ideas.

- Observing others and their actions can help a lot when there is a lack of creativity and innovation. It is an easy task to get indulged in observation sessions.

- Books can be treated as a factory of new ideas. The more you read, the more you will be able to use up your creative mind. This will ultimately result in the generation of some life-changing ideas.

Even if you feel that what you are doing right now in your life is actually great, there is nothing wrong with looking out for the better. Try visualizing your ideas with you in the picture and think about the outcome. Do not try to alter the reality of the same and try viewing them as they might turn out to be in reality. Also, traveling on the same path won't do any good for you. You can only come up with something new when you start walking on a different path.

So, if you are interested in the various aspects of innovation and the generation of ideas, scroll up and click the buy button now and have a great life ahead!